I0447311

Fantastic Mandala Coloring

Copyright: Published in the United States by Cathy Osterberg
Published December 2016
ISBN-13: 978-1541222717
ISBN-10: 1541222717

Thank you

www.ingramcontent.com/pod-product-compliance
Lightning Source LLC
Chambersburg PA
CBHW051946280526
45789CB00009B/3188